THE
CHICAGO
HOME

THE CHICAGO HOME

LINNEA JOHNSON
winner of the Beatrice Hawley Award

Alice James Books
Cambridge, Massachusetts
1986

Acknowledgments:

An earlier version of "Sandhill Cranes" appears in *Front Lines*, a collection of poetry with Campbell, Coleman, and Dean (Polemic Number One Press, 1983). The version of "Sandhill Cranes" in this book placed in the 1985 Billee Murray Denny Poetry Competition. Other poems from *Front Lines* included in this collection are "Walking Up the Champs-Elysees," "Because They Could Not Be Entirely Honest," and sections of the "Maria" poems. The complete text of the "Maria" poems appears in the Sornberger anthology, *All My Grandmothers Could Sing* (Free Rein Press, 1984). Other poems in this collection have first appeared in *Cottonwood Review, The Beloit Poetry Journal, Whole Notes, The American Poetry Review,* and *Prairie Schooner.* Others appear in *Adjoining Rooms*, a collection edited by Banset, Deal, Saiser, and Sornberger (Platte Valley Press, 1986).

Loving and special thanks to Meredith, Pat, Judith, Hilda, Janet, and Charlie and the many other people who so dearly advise and encourage.

The publication of this book was made possible with support from the National Endowment for the Arts, Washington, D.C., and the Massachusetts Council on the Arts and Humanities, a state agency whose funds are recommended by the Governor and appropriated by the State Legislature.

Library of Congress Catalogue Card Number 86-080006
ISBN 0-914086-62-6 (cloth)
ISBN 0-914086-63-4 (paper)

Alice James Books are published by the Alice James Poetry Cooperative, Inc.

Alice James Books
138 Mount Auburn Street
Cambridge, Massachusetts 02138

CONTENTS

THE CHICAGO HOME

CRAZY SONG

****

Father sings this one. He is visiting me. We are
across from one another. In my living room.
Mother is dead a thousand miles away.

You say it again: mama crazy. Thunderstorms
in her skinny head. Crazy. Not

crazy-in-love-with-you crazy. Not crazy
to-be-married-to-you-that-forever-long crazy.
Not crazy-like-a-fox crazy. Those
not what you mean.

You mean: a woman like *that* crazy crazy. You
say it again: mama crazy then. Flowerpots-
over-the-third-floor-porch crazy. The don't-
leave-me crazy. Jesus-singing-crazy-over-the-
railings-to-the-garages, the garbage cans,
the backyard-neighbors-who-listened
unlike you
crazy.

The quiet-as-a-mouse crazy. The saving-it-up-
until-you-were-trying-to-get-some-sleep-nights
crazy.

Crazy: Mama crazy.

Singing churchy tunes to the screaming wires: Mama
soldered to them. That kind of crazy.

Mama crazy, you say: no fault of yours.

****

Next Song: a descant. The fixed, known melody, the
psychiatrist. My mother's melody, pieces of the 27th
Psalm, a song of deliverance.

SOME WOMEN CAN GET THROUGH MENOPAUSE
PRETTY MUCH ON THEIR OWN even though those
women will at some point routinely need medication.
Even the best wife will turn into an annoying interfering
bitch who breaks out in whining and crying spells. If
infertility has been a problem, they become even worse.
Electrotherapy is often required; until then, try Miltown.

> the lord is my light and my salvation;
> whom shall i fear? the lord is the
> strength of my life; of whom shall i
> be afraid?

SOME WOMEN CAN GET THROUGH MIDDLE AGE
WITHOUT THE USE OF DRUG THERAPY, but even the
healthiest of middle-aged women are problematic to be
around. An effective therapy short of hospitalization is a
combination of psychiatric and tranquilizer therapy—to
soften the blows of middle-age for you, for everyone.

> though an host should encamp against me,
> my heart shall not fear; though war
> should rise against me, in this will i
> be confident.

SOME WOMEN CAN GET THROUGH THEIR ENTIRE
LIFE WITHOUT BEING A BURDEN to their husbands,
their families, and to themselves. When this is not the
case, try

hear, o lord, when i cry with my
voice: have mercy also upon me
and answer me.

SOME WOMEN IN THEIR MIDDLE YEARS PUT UP
QUITE A STINK WHEN THEY ARE IGNORED,
BELITTLED, OR PUT OUT TO PASTURE. We don't think
you should have to go through their little tantrums,
depressions, and spells. An effective therapy is often

hide not thy face far from me; put
not thy servant away in anger: thou
hast been my help; leave me not,
neither forsake me, o god of my
salvation.

****

This song played from memory. In the dark. Short
fingers on the keyboard. Opus 37.

She is straightening the shades.
It is Friday, her cleaning day, and this is
how she begins those Fridays. It is going to be
a hot one but she will open no window until dusk
and then only briefly, trusting nothing to night air.

Soon she will begin lifting each leaf of each violet,
left forefinger where leaf meets stem, right couple fingers
petting the dust off. She will check their soil before
she moves to the next whole plant, nip off
less thriving leaves, bloomed flowers. They are always
flowering, these violets: she is their season. I watch and sit

bored to tears before eight a.m. these summer mornings
of these gradeschool vacations
thinking her life is dull and she is more boring than even
her repetitive movements—the small, tiny care she takes
    for things.
I hate her and wish to be on my way, away, older than I
    am: not her.

Before I tune out for a day of marauding bike riding, far
into known regions, she will
ask me if I would like to have devotions with her. I will
say no.

When I return and before my father gets home from his
        work, she
will be practicing Sunday's hymns at her Hammond. She
will stop in time to boil and fry up hot food.

Before I leave with my mother for Friday night choir
        practice
my father will have read himself to sleep on the green
couch, bald head taking on the embroidery of her fine
couch pillows.

            ****
Song in which the refrain is even clearer than in
the first song, the refrain being, 'on my back.'

Though he is not speaking to me as much as
he is simply speaking, he tells me
as if we now had companion backs, he and I,

that she was always on it: She was always
on my back, my father says. Behind her back

he and what he calls 'the best in Chicago at the time'
shrink agrees

that his part
in this coming apart of hers
was that, if he had any part at all, he was too
nice: not one of those
men who knock women to their senses.

His face is clear of doubt, eyes clearer than
hers after the seven electrocutions I find out about
today. She was quiet at least after that. Off my back,
my father says ... though

six months later
she aggravated for something again
but by that time he'd learned something too,
fisting her a threat of a repeat wired-bed, saying:

Get off my back,

woman, or I'll send you back there again.

Didn't hurt a bit, that electric shock stuff, he says
now, as then. Says she settled right back down after that.
    No
problem though she was getting 'funny'

again right before she died. But he's better now.

His eyes begin to move around my room; I think
he wonders when I'll be starting lunch. He says
Remember when you two were always praying for me.

****

Marriage Pavane, that slow dance for couples at
court. My mother—made up from photographs she
left.

Camp Eleanor, 1939.
Close to her chest this summer
is the kind of bow arrows proceed from,
making her point into colored straw
a dozen yards from the arc her back makes,
the seersucker jumpsuit, the spread fingers.

This is the year before her marriage,
depression confined to those circular wells
on either side of her keen knees.

Penned on the white fluted border of this photo
is the place, the date,
and that her cabin's name was 'Phoebe': Stringbean
Lilly took the picture.

Reid Murdoch, 1936.
She has packed prunes here, now working
as a secretary. At her parents' home where she lives,
she keeps the music conservatory medals
in hankies in her underwear drawer. Saturdays

she fixes young fingers off and onto piano keys
the metronome competing with her father's mantle clock
for distaff, harmony,
half hours at a time.

In the kitchen the herring meets the brine.
Linens boil these mornings on a basement coal-fired stove.

Teaching music is not packing prunes. My mother
saves her conservatory compositions all of her life.
When they come water-packed, she buys Monarch Finer
        Foods,
plums, mostly—a Reid Murdoch enterprise. Her loyalty

continues in me; after she dies, I find a purple ribbon
for diving and put it in with the medals
I continue saving.

I count two dozen photographs of her
with the other Reid Murdoch women.

May 1947.
The wedding shower scrapbook has been put away
seven years, the baby shower scrapbook lies on top of it.
My mother adds to the weight loss the marriage began
forty pounds that first year, now twenty more from the
        care of

this baby. This baby which has come

out of the coldest Spring yet from the mis-
fortune of someone else. She watches it sleep,
keeping it from suffocation and draft, circling
its mouth for foreign objects. She has always

done what she has been told are the right things,
cried, then prayed, when she did not do them well
        enough:
this adopted child, a failure of her faith and the infertility
she assumed was her own:

A just God judging her. This photograph
has her holding me. Behind us, someone else tenses
in case that baby's head needs steadying. Or her thin, thin
arms go inexplicably slack.

MANY TIMES

It is night. She opens the large brown
door, the lemon light from the hall

following her in. One fairy tale,
one Bible story she'll read tonight
as every night until I will sometimes think

Jack the Baptist climbed beanstalks.
I watch her mouth from underneath, my head
on the thin, covered bones of her lap,

my braids thick as her arms. Mornings

I will find the suede tongue of a bookmark
at the end of the stories. She will

have read clear through to the ever afters
my head solid with sleep or not, such weight

nothing against such promise.

HOW COULD WE UNDERSTAND IT OTHERWISE

Here, in this museum of natural history
I sit cross-legged on buffalo hide
in this round, round place, this
eight pole earth lodge round
with a tunnel out, uterus and vagina

built here facing east
but with a pained sense of replication
about it — plastic pumpkin braids,
strings to keep us from the altar,
a floor of concrete, not mud.

The Pawnee boys, the museum guide says,
had to remain kind to their sisters
all the days of their lives: this is how

the guide explains the sense of matriarchy
to us. How could we understand it otherwise.

The sisters, the good, fast womenfriends
established such lodges by choosing
choosing each other,
then choosing the one man to combine with
to form her children. Here
the choice of these sisters, these women,

built communities, a culture: fifty people
she would choose to live in such a lodge
as this one. Divorce a matter of her
removing his things from the circle of things.

Lineage,
heritage traced through women's choices.

Among the daughter's things
are small tipis: How else could they
have understood so well the elements of construction
without having held such models

in their own hands as young girls.

The guide does not say
where the buffalo have gone, why
the Pawnee left eastern Nebraska, round lodges
like this one, this matriarchal culture

to live in plywood and flypaper desolation
on the outskirts and good graces
of the colonizing patriarchs

who now replicate even mud, pumpkin, women's choices
and the daughters' small tipis

as museum displays, forged artifacts,

where all can be explained, guided. How
could we understand it otherwise.

SANDHILL CRANES, PLATTE RIVER

I.
It is that time in the cycle of things
they are to return.

Nothing is like it was: I am thinner
in my belief in the routine progress of seasons
anymore, but we decide to drive the

hundred miles west to find the Cranes. You
are near to me as hope is to doubt and, today,
as distant. I think we will find

nothing. I mistake
empty sky for them — too early, they
do not fly this far east — then I point at geese:
you say, "no, those are geese." Then I hear their voices
entangled in the blank and greying sky where they are
        not.

Then, I see no evidence of them anywhere. A ten-thousand
        year
pattern broken: they are not here this year, I think.
Haltingly, I anyway assemble what I know of their past

migration, tell you they be red-headed,
coo something like distant pigeons. Simple
blocks, I say, from where we live, the zoo had one
we could have found, we could have seen.

II.
We drive the brown-grey roads platted into mile blocks
despite this river; we can find no road that runs with
it. We drive and drive and drive, criss-crossing the river,
    oh, twenty

times or more. I am convinced we will find nothing, that
    we are
here for no reason we can name. We leave

the car as if it, too, has betrayed us, crouch through
    thickets,
over unused wire fences, trample years of weeds and nests
    and leaves.

A milkweed pod still closed from a Spring ago surprises
    us
to open it as if such a thing had not before ever
been discovered. Thumb to thumb, you pry apart along
    the seam.
Still wet inside lie folded silks like unfurled feathers.

Upstream a thousand feet, the Cranes—
they move and call and fly.

TERMS OF SURVIVAL: WINTER STORMS

I.

It had never occurred to me that I would not survive.
Now, I see that possibility clear as washed ice,
stern as a sparrow frozen to its branch.

A poster tells me what I must do, what I must have already
    done
to live through one or another of these storms: I think
of all the things I have forgotten, resisted doing,
all the things which might have saved me
and which, few of them, have I done.

The cracks unpatched in roofs and walls, undone sealing
at the windows, wood I should have cut and logged and
    stacked
by now.

All those unprotected windows, the trees without their
    wrappings,
the unlocked doors, the unshut transoms, the unplugged
    saggings
of the basement walls,

the straggler cat I left outdoors and never saw again.

II.

The poster chills me through
though today it is warm enough; the house,
if not so firmly plastered, does stay put,
the straggler cat I can imagine lapping meat at another
    stoop.
All other deaths and loss
mend squalling at their uneven seams,
hooded with a sly protecting membrane. Until now.

And now I see the possibility that I will not survive
to refute these terms others give me—
to outlive the winter storms, the summer ones,
that strew my life.

But, today, blatant as a hungry sparrow, I vow to live
despite the lack of other posters
arming me with terms of how
to contrive around all the other things
out there alive to kill me.

WITH YOUR FATHER AFTER TWENTY-FIVE YEARS

You will sit down, bitter as arsenic, on the rind of your
    chair,
sit down with him and you will ask, "Where
have you been. All my life. I have been
better off
without you. How is it you can have left
me?
Stayed gone?"

He will sit on an opposing side of that which is between
    you,
rest elbows on the edge of it. He will sit there, large and
    old
— it has been twenty-five years —
his red cockfeathers still red though dusted now
with a greying maroon. He will sit there looking
or not looking at you,
the same cigarette you remember from the photograph
held at the same pitch,
held at that threatening angle to your eye; it
will watch you even if he does not.

You will want to say to him, for yourself,
for your mother: "I'm glad" (your face will clench
into a grin that could shatter glass) "I'm glad, glad, glad,
    glad, glad
glad as can be
glad you have been with me
no longer than you were. And why weren't you?"

There are ways in which your mother has sent you here
to avenge her, to lose you, too, as she has lost
these twenty-five years to the hating of him.
Effigy, he is no worse than anyone else's father.

He will order after you, ordering what you have ordered:
baked potato, sour cream and butter, a cut of meat. But
the wine will provoke you most. You fear you'll kill him
should you disagree; you will drink his wine,
cool and white like his fingers, and it will cut
the words from the walls of your throat. You will
like the wine.

You will remember the time in your mother's kitchen,
the time your eyes turned black, dilating
at the miscalculated thrust fist, his forearm bulging at you,
even the veins pulling it forward toward you.
You will say to yourself "but that's over now.
But it isn't. It doesn't matter. But it does."
The time you were two. Or one. Small.
That is not the only time he missed you like that.

You will watch him eat as if he were among friends.
"Where have you been? Your touch could have killed me
then," you will think. The cold coffeepot hangs in your
     memory
suspended still over your two-year-old skull.
He should bolt from the drinking of coffee,
you will think. But he will not.

He will be wearing no special markings; not a series of
     nines
and sixes, not ashes, not sackcloth. Horns worn to
     nubbins—
even his thinning hair will cover them. He will not wear
     your
baby shoes on gold ribbon around his neck. He will not

cross himself and kneel when he sees you. There will be
nothing telltale written in red on his shirt.
He will be sorry for nothing. There will be no traceable
thread
of ruin to glitter for you in his life. He will have been
spared cancer or will have recovered from it. Any diabetes
will be under control. He will be nothing
if not ordinary. This seventy-year-old man
will be sorry for nothing; should he say it,
you would not believe him.

With a face like your own, he will be across from you.
You will ask him the questions other women have asked
their fathers, say the things other women have said
to their fathers. You will say, "I hate you.
Why? Did you never! Love me,
my mother?"
You will add, as you see him bite small pieces from his
meal,
"Why?"

You will want to spend some of your mother's last
twenty-five
years on him,
your mother who is in the glint in your eye, the sweat,
cold as his wine, running into puddles at your feet—
the mother who is you and not you.
He will like you or not like you no matter what you say.
It will be, finally, good that you have gone, seen him.

26.

Leaving, you will remember the answers to your questions,
your questions, your answers. You will leave
and it will be your mother
you will cry for.
Though you have tried, your mother will not,
will not come along with you on these questions,
these answers. She spends her vision
hating this two-year marriage of a man,
this man who deserves the attention of curiosity
once over dinner and no more.
He is an uncut skeleton key
among uncut skeleton keys.

Leaving, you will have fulfilled no prophecy, loosed no
        devils,
met no one you could not have met in a bar any night of
        any week,
made no irrevocable choices, denied or made no
        allegiance,
killed no one, birthed nothing.

He will say, "I loved you. I loved your mother."
He will be telling the truth.

BECAUSE THEY COULD NOT BE ENTIRELY HONEST

And I say to you: it takes no special courage to lie.
You know this: it is not news

Just a given, you say, some price extracted.

We talk of Cather, her Ántonia, her Alexandra,
the choices she denies them
which she did not deny herself and you tell me
not to be harsh with her,
with you,
for her living in the bosom of a woman
yet for not daring the edge of things:
not writing those frontiers, those pioneers,
but the other ones instead.

I say: Being a woman is the primary fact — the *prima facie*
    case
they have against us.
Reason enough is that we are women, eye to eye.

You shiver that I could judge so,
that I demand of you, of myself, of other women
that boldface courage which, we both know,
could get us unloved or killed, asked to leave,
    unpublished,
flung from pride and down the stairs at dad's.

You say to me: But you have always lived on the front lines
and I say: We all do
It is simply a matter of recognizing it.

If disguises weakened Cather's work, or yours, or mine,
how much more do they weaken lives: because they could
    not be
entirely women.

I care not who calls me 'woman'
or the other names.
I embrace the name and myself and you,
call myself 'woman' first in a roaring which
I have heard you use,
a roaring which calls us all together
our bold faces turned to one another
across whatever distance is left between us.

BURNING PASSION

In Milwaukee he teases her with kerosene
and a match. A joke. She has not

lashed him naked to a chair
rope gouging his flesh he beats with alcohol
to see it open, tighten, redden. She has not thrown him
down the stairs fifteen years and three miscarriages in a
    row
just to know how it feels. Again and again

she has not pumped booze and loathing fierce up his
    body,
punched eyes, breasts, that offending smile

summoned from god knows what flickering at the lips. No.
This man's joke over ninety-five percent of her body,
funny as his sex is to her love, is, here and now,

a crime of what is called passion. One more
beer-burping wife joke. This man

watched his t.v. one evening, saw a woman
kerosene a sleeping husband

who had
lashed her naked to a chair, rope expanding tight
gouging into the red scream of her flesh. Had
thrown her down stairs fifteen years and three
    miscarriages
in a row. Had pumped at her—loathing, fierce, and
    boozy—
punching her eyes, her breasts

and that offending smile
soon to be frozen swollen, her mouth nearly emptied of
    her teeth.
Finally, a match for him.

But it is a man
who watches one woman defend herself
and then he kills another woman, a wife. A joke. Did you
    hear
the one about the guy in Milwaukee...

DAFFODILS

The deepness of this night is heavy hands pressing and I
am out in the deepest of it with scissors
to cut from the ice, my daffodils, persistent as thunder,
this night of lightning and snow,

this frost, the breath of a long dead friend up my neck.

Persistent as thunder, but they are dying, these daffodils,
against all odds that they should be able to live,
this being the middle of an April.

They lose. I drop my scissors.
I have cut them, cut them all
to lie in my arms, dead
like starlings, heads to unrelenting panes.

I take them inside anyway, run stems
as well as my hands, which refuse to warm,
into the warm, warm water.

Still, I prop them, dead, and more obviously so, into
this vase I have prepared for them. But they are dead,
what green in their stems is not better than opaque,
petals papery as burned skin.

I wish I had built a fire tonight. My hands will
not warm. I have left the scissors out in the ice and I
will not sleep until morning.

WALKING UP THE CHAMPS-ELYSEES:
ON KEEPING A NOTEBOOK IN PARIS

This isn't my first trip, won't be my last, legs still
covered over with their winter growth, notebook
clutched like the coupon keeper I use
in the A & P back home. Back in the
States.

Today my food stamps ache in my wallet like devalued
francs. Where is my child
that she keeps running out into the street like that?

I am in Paris with all my heart and soul
though the faint licking of puddle water at my sneakers,
at my socks, tells me something else. This notebook
is brown sacks from the A & P: more than
I should have taken
for the fifty cents of kidneys
I got in my other hand.

This place
stinks like Chicago and I want
to be in Paris writing
songs, cheese labels, letters home to my dead-life
children, postcards, notes on cafe-soaked napkins,
riddles to delight myself with in my taffeta dotage,
stories, poetic renderings of my
life. My life

and the lives of other hairy-legged women, coupons
kept to keep us warm. My life
is in a notebook in Paris
no matter what.

My children keep the streets from having nothing to do.
It rains in Chicago all spring.

SHE HAS NEVER KNOWN

She has never known when to leave well enough alone,
when to take the charm out into the marketplace
and buy groceries with it: celery for a week's soup,
scrap meat for her dinner. She has never learned, for
    instance,
to buy millet for cakes. She refuses to learn this, buying it
    instead
for the bluejays, for the shy cardinals, even for the grackles
which peck at her ears as she will sit in the snow to talk
    with them.
Her hands know only to warm the ice from her peach
    tree, her plum,
even the mulberry which grow wild as she does
in the weed patch she calls her yard.

She will never learn: she has been told this.
She has never known
that her province is smaller than she thinks it is,
that there is no wonder or magic in the decay of the old
    things
she fills her old house with: that to save the log with the
    squirrel-stored
nuts is to deny her house heat: nothing more.

With the charm she could buy shoes for her children,
swaddling for the littlest one who now roams everywhere
naked as the peaches on her summer tree. She could
    exchange
the charm for all that she now makes; she could hear
    music
other than that those birds make, for instance.

34.

She will not listen. She will not know
that there is more to a charmed life than the charm.

Instead, she will take the charm,
holding it sometimes in her mouth to touch the designs
    on it:
sometimes she can read the year it was made with her
    tongue.
For some reason, which escapes everyone else, she laughs
when she does this, her eyes falling behind her rising
    cheeks
like sunsets in open country.

BESIDE ME

Beside me
with one of her headaches
she says, "draw me
a picture" and squirms.
Unborn, she has attended me
these past soup-kitchen years,
these years of baldhead bones in water
draining in and out of me,
in and out of the children
who are here
who sleep like night fires
in opposite rooms.

I explain to her there are no pictures
in me tonight, inks dry,
dried as the bones, paper thin,
thinner than pale water,
thinner than the last
shallow-breathed years.

She is not satisfied and hrumphs
wanting nothing less than the picture
she wishes I were drawing. She says,
"I didn't ask for no soup
story or no bone story."

"Listen," I say, but she fades,
wanting the crayola purple-pink skies,
the Tenniel-outline Alice in blues, the
greens of some warm tree swamp steaming
with gold wings, the ache of a blood color,
some glass shard silver bird
sitting full center
in the wake of a froth-white dawn.

Gone, I finger the place she has last sat.
I have sometimes, like tonight,
named her Kathryn, a name of my own,
after the little girls we have all given away
for no less reason than this.

MARIA OF THE HOME FOR WAYWARD ENFANTES

Maria of the Home for Wayward Enfantes, 1949.

It could have meant 'princess'
had I been speaking French,
had anyone else. No one was.
Simple, 'enfante' meant
infant. Except in my case,
Maria says, where it also meant
howling white iron beds
at the shift change.

Don't any of you say "aw"
now.
I don't want to hear it,
Maria says. Where were you
when it counted. A parentless
infant is a parentless infant.

I just want you to know
I noticed.

Maria and Her Friend, Angela. They're Pals. 1957.

A thousand light years from her house
Maria cries, pants down with Angela
in high weeds. Sunflowers are the only friendly
faces looking at either of them right now.

There's one bruise here that looks like Florida,
Maria says. And glass. She holds a doming
nipple to her friend's grey mouth.

On Tuesday, they find a nest of burned baby
somethings. They eat red berries for a week
and don't go home.

At The Funeral, Maria's Uncle Tells A Joke. 1958.

Herb and Edna lie '69' in matching caskets
at the business end of St. Catholic's church.
Herb's brother, Bill, says, one arm like a leg
around the redundantly orphaned Maria, "Wa
duy ya do wit a dead dog at night.

Ya take him for a drag."

Maria wants to go to the movies; she settles
for some cake at the soft churchlady's hand.

Later, Bill will remember
orphan tears are good luck; he'll
say so, gripping around Maria to her nubling breasts.

Maria and Angela: They Talk. 1959.

Maria wants to know what it's like
to be that blond and to have a sister,
one you didn't borrow, at that.

Angela says tomorrow they're gonna
get a kitten: Adopt it, just like you,
Angela says.

Maria runs for home, gets lost
and spends the afternoon ringing doorbells,
hoping for a good guess.

Bill Turns Into Maria's Daddy. Judge's Chambers. 1960.

Two rooms over Harry's on the southwest side of
Chicago and all the beer Milwaukee makes. Bill says
orphans got no sense of humor. He likes poker better.
Ha. Ha.

Maria Hits It Big At Sweet Sixteen. 1965.

This guy who looks like a cabbage says Maria's
pretty. He wants to take her pitch-ure. She says
she's never heard that one before, but her face,
which looks like weeds to her, turns up like some
bright flower to a morning sun. She signs right off,

asks Bill to do the same for her. He says, don't
break that asshole's camera before he pays ya. He'll
be down at Harry's if she wants him.

Two Polaroids and a Brownie later
this guy says he bets Maria's prettier
from even her thick waist
down
and why don't she let him see.
His magazine ain't payin' to see what daylight sees.

By dawn she's got herself to Angela's
who punches her a good one
for how can she go and be
so goddamn dumb.

Without Angela, There is No One to Talk to. 1967.

Without Angela, there is no one
to talk to.

Maria Strikes A Compromise. A Long Night. 1967.

I.
Maria walks home, palms taut across the tops of pickets
thinking, well, now she's pregnant too and
in no better shape for it than her idea-of-a-mother
was for it those eighteen years ago
when it was Maria's turn
to be the live worm in the bean.

She hopes that if her hand starts ripping
it'll be a sign, tell her what to do.

Maria says, it could be worse, was
for Angela, her pal. It could be worse,
Maria says.

No one is listening.

II.
A compromise, Maria says, is when everyone
agrees to lose, but Maria can't even seem
to find herself one of those tonight
between those hangers she has heard about

and the orphanage
which no one will believe
Maria still remembers.

Though what got Angela was some skinny garden hose
that didn't work, her aunt's old worn out Hoover
and two hours at the Stop Inn Motel
with a Dran-O douche
that did.

A Long Night. Maria Goes To The Movies. 1967.

Maria goes to the movies tonight,
lifts herself onto that screen
like she was that low-cut satin number
half-worn by that big, big woman up there,

that woman
waiting to be slung under some ol' silky man and
ridden halfway to heaven
without the consequences.

Maria has always looked for her mother
in movies. Tonight she wants
so bad to be near her. Maria
sits through the movie
until she knows all the words.

A Longer Night in 1967.

Bill shows up home wearing pissed
like six fur coats in summer. He says
he's heard: been drinking with the priest.

By morning, a zillion years from now,
Maria won't be pregnant anymore.

Maria Wakes Up Three Nights Later. Still 1967.

She's been away forever
wrapped against the cold in barbed wire coats,
bloody knives banging at her emptied waist,
nipples pinching in revolving doors, head soaked
in liquid iron...

I'll be good, I promise, mommy.
Tombstone angels fall on Maria's chest
like gargoyles off bombed churches.

Downstairs, the place is stuffed
to the ceiling and up the legs of Maria's bed
with brine cigars, burning fat, and salami men
playing Bill like some guys play guitar.

The noise is water you could drown in.

Maria tells her Angela she'll leave
right now with her
if she will fast teach her how to swim
or fly.

Maria Says She's Found Love. 1979.

Maria says she's found love
thirty years after she'd spent
her first six months
rolling around white iron beds
with no visible means of being purported
to be anyone's kid.

She says she loves ya
and she'll mean it
until the first time you take it back
in any of the little ways
people usually do. Like

waiting too long between her question,
"You love me,
dontcha?"

—no rhetorical questions for Maria—

and your being cute, wrinkling up your nose and
saying, "Gee, I don't know."

Maria will be gone fast as her mother
got away from her, her father from her mother
before that. Though

Maria says
things is diff'rnt now.

Danny Tells Maria What It's Like To Be A Man. 1980.

Danny tells Maria
That's what it's like
to damn well be a man—
his finger points a hit fist
clear through her head—

She'd better learn that much
and quick...this courtroom's not his idea
of a good damn time.

The judge confines him
to her attorney's questions
and listens like a brother. Maria sits
like laundry in her chair. Danny says
it's his damn business, anyway. Gotta
break 'em to the bridle early on.
Their heads all nod

44.

except Maria's
which still aches from Danny's last time
smackorama a couple weeks before:

"It's the last time, I promise
you Maria. Come on now,
lemme in."

This afternoon in court
wears thin as skin about to give way
to a fist. And then
it's over:

They parole him to her like another marriage.
Maria's husband is a loaded gun—all registered
and legal.

YOUR MOTHER

For what ails you
there isn't one: no cure.

No Curie out there killing herself
to discover one for you, either. Sorry

for yourself with your reasons.
Nothing remembers you better than old habits.

You have been hating her all of your life. She
is who you have wished dead since you have been
tall enough to reach your bedroom doorknob to slam
the first of many doors in her face. She is

your reluctance, your persistence, the reason
you bake no cookies, bake them incessantly, why
you cry in the night or have never learned to...

and now she is old,
older even than you thought she used to be. She

has given up tacking your artwork to her refrigerators,
she wants nothing more of your wet pants or doll arms,
truck tires, rants about the buying of your luxuries,

herds of your peers, your offspring which you wield
through her home. She will patch nothing more of yours,

going off not even noticing the rips and tears and worn
    things
you drag to her still.

Lucky for you she is this old and really will die
soon. You can attend her funeral, help pay for it
maybe
cry your eyes out

leave wondering why she never loved you enough.

CHICAGO, IN COOK COUNTY: CHILD SAVING

The Chicago Nursery and Half Orphan Asylum, The Audy
Home, The Chicago Foundlings Home, The Catharina
Kaspar Industrial School for Girls

saved children, salvaged the fingers of girls

into the cheap labor of sock-knitting, shuttled them
into the weaving of woolens, into the pressing of
someone else's fine, fine linens.

The Volunteer Rescue Army Children's Home, Saint
Vincent's, The Ruth and Eleanor Clubs, The Chicago
Home for the Friendless. Women and Children's
Hospital   all

saved
children, industry impressed early
into the palms and arms and shoulders of the unclaimed,
        unremitting children of the friendless
poor, dead, committed
and unable. Saved

into the industrial foundling hospitals and homes
and schools and clubs, into the business of
learning an imposed trade, the learning of
one's place. Conduct, according to Matthew Arnold

and the others, being three-fourths of life,
that remaining quarter
those sawed-off bits of gratitude for the salvaged
industrious

learning, learning, learning the cleansing of the
hexagonal tiles of someone else's bathroom floors.

SLIGHT LECTURE TO THE YOUNG MAN ON MY LEFT

I.
She has touched your hair in a public place, remaining
        too long, perhaps
on the thick of it as it curves the back of your head. She
        was thinking
later, of touching it again.
In the sunlight this time. That sunlight
like too many people, you say,
(she hopes you have told her she is not one of those
        people)
pushing at you, wearing their needing like motley.

You wonder why if she needs nothing from you
she cares to stay, to stay, to linger with you
like bright sunlight which—you are amazed—dazzles her
as it moves like her fingers through your hair.

She wants you, she says, and you wonder what for.

II.
You have met her today to tell her
that if you love her, it is too bad for you.

You have come, pack mules behind you, full with trunks
        full of clothes,
pickaxes for the precipices you see yourself on,
implements and apparel for the wrong season,
for a region of the country
she is not in,
has no use for.
You have prepared for a trek through dangerous terrain.

You imagine things running away with you. Her. Trains.
Running away from you. Her.
Thick, heavy, plummeting trains
you run for
while you run away.

You have met her today wearing your leather aviator's
        helmet, that long scarf
like the one Isadora wore her last ride in the Masarati.
Under the thick hide, there is chainmail:
shirt and trousers
and a lover's heart done up, trussed
pushing at you
as she is not
(she says: do what you like)
pushing at you, now slipping out.
You are afraid if she sees it
she will stop laughing at your getup
and begin laughing at you.

She also asks you home with her
and she is not laughing
but smiling, seeing something break through
which, though she will not tell you, reminds her
of a countryroad sunset you saw together once.

III.
And it is not that I will, any more than will she,
tell you your alternatives, lay them before you like so many
        ponds full of goldfish,
and I will not lecture you on the allaying of fears, the
        mornings you have yet
to hold together.

I will not tell you anything more than she has, than you
        have
told yourself, these fancies of her you have,
these days you have spent with her without telling her.

And I will not show her to you now: she is probably
    bathing anyway,
candle on the hamper, sandalwood soap easing her body,
    singing to herself
small tunes
perhaps some of them are of you, perhaps not.
Later, though not much,
she will ease herself between sheets, her back to her wall,
pillows around her as if she were in a snowbank,
as if to hold through to the next day,
a day she fears as little as she fears you.

But I will tell you this:
there are things you must leave
if you choose to find her porch, her stairs,
your way up to her even breathing,
the sight of her, fresh-waked, seeing you find her—
and it is the same for both of you
(I will convey these things to her in the morning when she
    will listen to me):
You must leave
back there with the packmules, pickaxes, and armour
the notion you have ever done this before.
Because you haven't. Not her with you,
not you with her.

A LESSON IN POMEGRANATES

What would I know about such things had I never
held their weight, curious, and curious,
taken one home, put an edge to it

and, wanting to know all
about what ever was there,
split it thoroughly

then and there on the board,

the corpus red from the wanting, the weight,
the splitting open of the thing itself. Of course,

one should know, there are some
not worth the taking. They resist all opening,

skins red as the others' but hard as poor bark.
What is inside them

is not worth the wanting, a comfort
in certain disappointment. Where they should be

all juice and eager because of it,
they are, instead, pale, to themselves,

pomegranates to the untrained eye
only, their substance making them unworthy
of their name.

MENU FOR A SNOWY AFTERNOON

                                         You call, and
what I want
begins in the remembering of meat, white as a throat
uncurling onto our forks from out the red shell.

A thousand miles of snow between us,
I tell you of enormous cold
pressing through walls
on its way into my bones. I have

nothing I want here. The tea you suggest,
I have run out of. You do not remember that lobster,
you quote me Stendhal regarding winter's bare branches,
tell me of the afternoon and the cherrywood fire

you have for yourself.
You wish I were with you.

In my refrigerator lies an out of season nectarine,
bananas past the eating, and the sharp, stark
hollows of a bony chicken, the afternoon

tightening into a winter night
in which to go hungry.
                                 I am out of everything
I want. Can not settle on what—no milk, no butter—
I have.

ONE MORE DAVID

The eighth race made it all untrue.
Up like a print on better paper from last ass in the gate,
he ran the stretch, took that far turn solid
and made for home and history never touching ground:
    One More David,
twenty-two to one.

As of that last half length, I have no longer lost
on every David
I ever strapped a hope to.

But, this one was no David
who, kneeling tit to tit with me
in the backseat of his Daddy's late-teen Olds,
found the inside of my thigh hot as a pancake one mid-
    December
and later kicked clear through the rear side steel door.

This time, this was no David
home from the Prom or to his wife
weeping fine-grained tears or big ones
about his mother, father, all his aunts,
his children, wife, or collie who'd be so
o, so disappointed in him. If they knew.
Dead laboratory rabbits or boyfriend at his side,
I wouldn't tell them, would I?

This, of all the overstuffed caged birds and empty barns of
    Davids,
the wound and scab of them, the sweet swift streak of one,
the pop cap, summer sky, wet nose, fruit basket,

dug-up corpse, milky eye, and pork chop,
dimwiddy, knuckle-sandwich, fish bait, dropped stitch,
herniated angel, limp fish, quart of ooze,
manna-mouthed, ripped page from Kant,
gnat-ass, carbuncle, salmon steak,
mosquito bite, singed hair of them—
This one, this one,
the one longshot of all the Davids
I bet right.

This time, a thoroughbred,
back broad as a stream and twice as fast,
this one,
a forty-seven forty payoff for my last two scraggly bucks,
ran for, not at me,
and not away.

SHE MIGHT HAVE RUN OFF INTO THE NIGHT
HEDGES

I.

She might have run off into the night hedges, the day lilies
with the fluttering leaves of the manuscript, her back
    glittering
broad and strong, tensed as if she had refused a chill
or were taking another lover.

I will call her Ann though her name is also Judith
or my name, Kathryn, or your name on your best days:
Ann might have run off writing
to London or from it, head and spirit ruffled,
trousers rolled to garters at her knees.

Perhaps the darkest night found her in New York,
this Ann, always writing,
moon-faced, catching what light there was,
what lover there was in the writing.
Writing rings around her fingers,
married ten times and more fiercely this way
than even had she been a mossy nun
or wife.

At times perhaps this writer-Ann would find
a pen, a stick and sand, the mimeo machine at church:
writing, always writing
running lickety-split feet white
bare to the ice glazing cobbles, bricks,
concrete to the eyes of those who refuse her,
her fluttering leaves,
once, twice, more times.

Until, writing, the shoes wear thin, then off.
Her lover, the leaves of her manuscript,
running off with her, away with her
into hedges or London or you

Or you.

II.
I warn you with this story
and although the ancient warmth of this Fall afternoon
fires your skin like clay in a kiln, your
hair all leaf-colored to my eyes, your thighs
like horses waiting in barns, I say, I warn you

I warn you of the life we Anns live
a life of pens and inks and sheaves of paper

taken to our beds like lovers who want us,
want to know us, lovers on which we leave ourselves
that paper taking our impressions
like bare earth takes rain.

Tonight and all nights, really, the nights
of all the Anns and Judiths and Kathryns
we spend in paper arms.

Just last night I passed palm over nipple,
mine, yours: I had written you
and taken you to bed.

III.
All the lives we Anns and Judiths and Kathryns have lived,
pens in our hands, bared feet and soles to the hardness

striking our lives like rocks at a stoning, running away
into the night, the day,
wearing out our shoe leather, our welcome,
the qualities that would have kept us safely linked
to our own families' eyes, the snug treachery of the
     convent,
the uneasy death of tract homes, the tugging, moaning
     chords
of voices like yours,
your satin back, the rills of your chest—

I will deny you until you go away.

CROSSCUT AND CHAINSAW

The crosscut handsaw is mine; I have brought it
from the chew of birch, the swift felling of willow,
the hot ache of an old oak dead two winters
outside my city windows, crying for the blade to lay it
     down.

Yours would as soon tear through my limbs
as the wood we walk to find, could cut the tires off your
     pickup
at fifty miles an hour, howls through air
eating its own screams to increase velocity.

I am in love with you from the neck down
looking for firewood from a finished orchard:
its seasoning will outlast our own. Today,

the give of leaf loam, the sky blue enough to die from,
the blaze of these Fall woods link us one hand each,

the other of our hands to our saws. I do not know
how you love me but I do know you are wrong
about the wood and how to cut it.

TUESDAY EVENING: FRONT PORCH

Your great silken doe-eyes have come, newly showered,
seeking—a note from your wife—release, absolution:
It is as if some mommy-person has bow-tied your neck
for this errand all of you must do.
All of you but your eyes relinquish me
to the brittle of your children,
your armchair wife.

Those brittle children stand fierce as sharpened pickets
between us; they want you home to daddy.
You explain this with your mouth from the far side of
        their fence,
your great eyes holding all of us loved, traveling my eyes,
aching for some glint of hardness to dismiss you,
to hold as oyster, sand, this sad forthcoming winter
of your encroaching age.

But your eyes, your eyes,
your great eyes come here tonight
sent out this night of pelting rain
from the comfort of an armchair wife
who loves you—you are amazed—with the suddenness
of this summer, brow-furrowed storm
to make a choice where none need be made.

If, as you say, she has your youth all sutured up inside her,
I, bare toes to the porch, say I, too, have spent mine
silly as new pennies in gum machines.

There is nothing you need retrieve: no matter.
I ask you as you are tonight
inside
for as long as your silken, doe-eyes cover me this way—
Like the fine soft light of the moon moving gentle,
coming from behind the breaking storm.

AND NOT TO KEEP

you have asked
the same questions three nights in a row. I

have answered it the other two. I ask

why you ask again

if I love you. Outside, the breeze changes
to wind as if calling a good rain to join it
this night which will turn furious
against all sides of every shelter. Inside,

we are silent, you and I. It is not the
simple question I think you have asked. "Yes"
kindles nothing for you. You are not asking

what I am answering

when I say that, yes, I love you. You want
more.

I say, love is not a quantity for me
I can give you no

'more'. It is like this as the rain begins,
a rain I would be out in like a tree

were we not damp inside,
the fire you attempt lighting impossible,
all wood damp or wet. The question

you want to ask me is
will you love me when the wood dries out,
when the storm stops, next time

one of us wants a fire in the stove.

I give you no answer you can take home with you
to stack or store or burn
cold nights when you are not with me, I with you.

I am of no more comfort to you
than this stack of damp wood
which I will burn when it dries out
for fire and not to keep

one night when you might not be here
and I would love a fire.

VACATION

Day One

We leave. I keep records as though I were my mother.
Odometer. What I pay for gas and how many gallons.
Where I buy what. Everything in me wishes
she were here, that this were one of those vacations
I rode feet to the glass in the backseat
watching lickety-split sky out the curvy back window.

These first fifty miles,
me riding a sullen shotgun under darker skies
upfront, next to you, I miss her; missing her
is ice in my spine spiraling around me.

I count and record.

Out past your face, the Loup River
stays with us for hours.

We stop for lunch: it is cheese and meat
on pumpernickel. Hardtack and whipped butter.
Diet Squirt. Apples. It is cold. We eat
and eat. You are wearing most everything
you brought with you for this week,

this week without constraint. Wool in May.

With me is my mother and with her
the sadness that lives in crevices
crying at the odd moments. I ignore

that you have not spoken, are waiting for me
to replace the family you have always spent
vacations with.

It becomes a passenger in this car,
that we are together like this.
We go farther west, north, away
into this vacation.

Before we sleep at the Keeney Motel in Halsey,
we read to each other, not talking yet. Two hundred eighty
     nine
miles, I say, from our houses to this
place.

I lie away from you and cry for my mother,
my daughter, all I have lost. I spend this night
losing sleep, walking the dark, dark room between us.

Day Four

Yesterday was the sixteenth of May—Marie Antoinette's
     two hundred
thirtieth wedding anniversary. Someone on the news is
     still
remembering. We

have talked. The rain sounds like soft gravel
on the car windows. There has been forecast snow
for the foothills we are entering. For the past

four days, what hasn't been closed has been
impossible, fogged over, rained out.

Over a rushing spring is a pergola. We put on orange
plastic and for a while we watch stones through silvery
     water.

We hold hands, kiss. Later, we see a bluebird,

find a hangnail of a hotel. It has a headboard which holds
our books, the candy bag.

We set up the coffeemaker for the morning.
The room fills instantly with smells I can remember
from mornings we have held like caught breath.

I see lines on your face I have not noticed before,
trace them with a light finger, hold you
tight like a compress to an ache.

We have walked the town, the river, through this rain.
We talk.

Day Five

We are in Custer County, South Dakota: It is where
        eastern and
western foliage and fauna meet, live together, encroach
        and recede.

Lightning set fires burn off pines, then grasses;
they grow in each others' places depending.

This morning's rain is a fine mist settling on our faces,
a satin over the five days
which we wear visible to one another.

Beneath our feet everywhere is cave.

I have been to this cave, Wind Cave, before
on a vacation with my mother, my father.

Today four of us descend with a guide, those other
two married fifty years, repeating today their honeymoon
      tour of this cave.
She walks with us. We wonder, silent as this dark, where
we will be in forty-eight and a half years.

I think in this perfect fifty-seven degrees
of the secrets beneath things: things you know of me,
I of you, what lives in me like the caves in South Dakota,
intimacies that run like streams underground. What it
      means

for us to have held hands in an open park, to have kissed
concerned only about the rain. To be here today with this
woman and her man, married together. I promise myself
      much today

and lag behind, move away from the others, from you, and
      wish again
for my mother. This time, I wish I had buried her in the
      side of a

limestone mountains and forever after dreamed
her sailing around such boxwork, silver-blue grottoes,
      undergound
lakes. Sioux legend says life in the form of bison

comes from a hole in the earth where the wind blows. I
      catch up with
you, my hand remembering the full weight and press of
      yours.

Day Seven

We have returned early,
me to my house, you to yours.

I return to a sense of living alone
with my cats, my daughter. I sit away from the rain
on my front porch, resting a teacup on my lap. We have

67.

talked,

held one another, kissed, all of it but
not long enough. Not long enough to keep us through
this vacation: I think today there is not enough talk,

not enough words to bridge, to mesh, to cement, to weave

us together. No matter what we want.
I rest my head, my shoulders, my back
against the slatted side of this house as I have rested against you.
This morning I wish I were my mother,

Marie Antoinette, the married woman in the cave. I

am not. Neither of us are.

My shoulders feel like iron.
I determine to find you this afternoon and to continue,
continue together

Against the clear pattern of this vacation.

THIS BEACH

I.
She has become, in a sense, replete, dimensional,
turning round herself to look and look again.

It has not been a year yet, but she is certain
it will be soon

and with that certainty, there exudes from her
the sense of a white Spring-morning room
opening passionately just beyond the thundering bouquet
    of lilac,
sand, and beach, and open sea

which, to her, means everything.

II.
She who has brought the lilac into the room
brings with her self surprise and the quick cryings

of one who, at one time, was convinced, in turn it was
impossible to be happy, impossible to be anything but.

She, too, has spent these months turning herself around,
moving, for the first time, for hours at a time,

just at the moment where closed and open meet: the
    doorway,
this beach, open water.

III.
At this moment, the blue from the sky, from the sea
reflect into the room
the white reflects out:

Together, they are everything.

YELLOW PINE TREE POEM FOR MY DAUGHTER, MORGAN

Thinking of you, my daughter, and the puzzlements
of age and size, how like me you are and how different
that alone makes you, I walk this yellow January day,

sun, a furious light interrupting the remarkable
smallness of the usual grey winter day, and I think

and I think, watching my feet walk and walk,
forgetting to look beyond them

until the light changes and I look up: there,

a hundred yards away, a lodestar yellow pine

two hundred feet taller than you and I together,
roots sunk past dirt, sand, and water, the aquifer
and rock, old bones and pottery, bricks, clay, oil,
shale, eons, myth, and history. Nothing small about her.

Nothing young or small. Even humiliated to lumber,
she would become ships, ties, girders, beams. Her round
weight would make things big, grand, make events and
    places

possible. The glitter of this day sounds through her
like the sea, wide water, ocean free from constraint and
    beach.

She can live anywhere and command more space and sky
than anything around her, translating always what things
    above
will mean to things around her.

We are like that tree, you and I, large and
even in your chestnut-yellow-haired youngness, old and strong,
and commanding. The tree is not there so that others may
see it and neither are we. She is different from the other trees around her.

I celebrate never having noticed any of this before.
I walk taller, larger, older, bigger going home
to tell you all of this in the yellow light of burning
logs which keep us warm all nights in all Januaries.

POETRY FROM ALICE JAMES BOOKS